W9-BHU-327

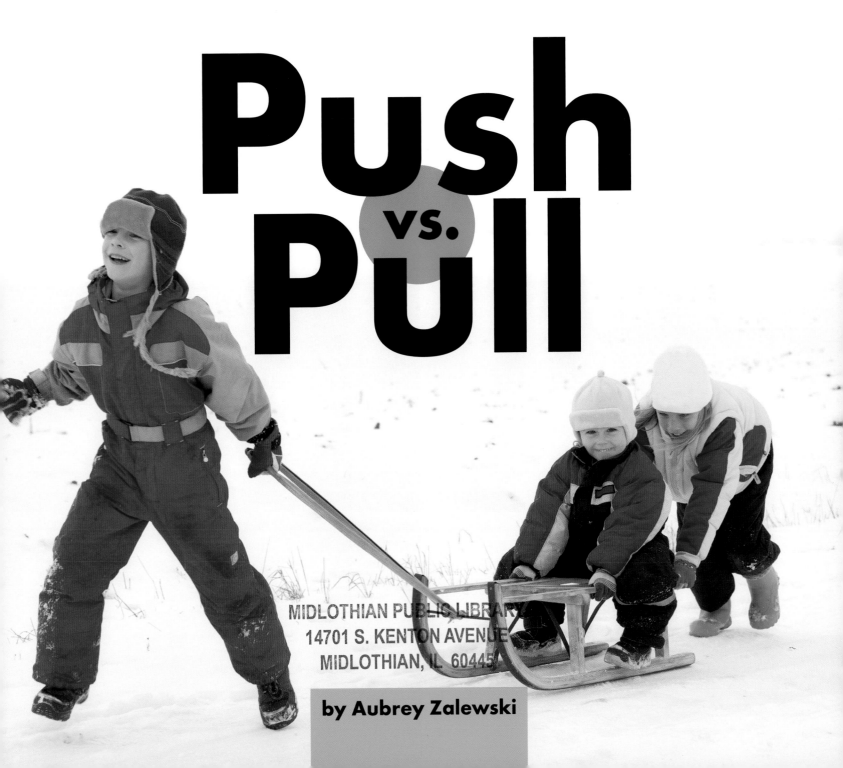

Push
vs.
Pull

by Aubrey Zalewski

The Child's World®
childsworld.com

Published by The Child's World®
1980 Lookout Drive • Mankato, MN 56003-1705
800-599-READ • www.childsworld.com

Photographs ©: Daniel M. Nagy/Shutterstock Images,
cover, 1; Monkey Business Images/Shutterstock
Images, 5; Shutterstock Images, 6, 13, 20; Anna
Berdnik/Shutterstock Images, 9; iStockphoto, 10;
JPL/NASA, 15; Lane V. Erickson/Shutterstock
Images, 16; Tressie Davis/Shutterstock Images, 19

ISBN 9781503844407 (Reinforced Library Binding)
ISBN 9781503846647 (Portable Document Format)
ISBN 9781503847835 (Online Multi-user eBook)
LCCN 2019956607

Printed in the United States of America

About the Author

Aubrey Zalewski edits and writes children's books. Aubrey spends her free time enjoying nature, baking goodies, and reading books. Aubrey lives in Minneapolis, Minnesota, with her husband and pet rabbit.

TABLE of CONTENTS

CHAPTER ONE

Pushing and Pulling

Ben's family is moving. Every box has to go on the truck. There are a lot of boxes. Ben wants to help. He tries to lift a box. It is very heavy. He pulls and pulls. He cannot lift it. But that will not stop him. He moves to one side of the box. Then he pushes against it. He pushes as hard as he can. The box begins to move. When Ben gets to the truck, his older sister comes to help. Together, they pull up on the box to lift it onto the truck's ramp. Ben pushes the box up the ramp while his sister pulls. They will have everything packed in no time!

Moving heavy boxes requires a lot of pushing and pulling.

PUSH

PULL

A **force** is a push or pull that can put an object in motion. When Ben pushed on the box, he was using force. Force happens when two objects interact. The force acts on both objects. Pushing moves objects away from the force. Pulling moves them toward it. Ben pushed the box away from him. When his sister helped move the box, she pulled it toward herself.

Force has both strength and direction. The box Ben pushed was heavy. He needed a strong force to move the box to the truck. The way he pushed the box was the direction of the force. Forces can be both **horizontal** and **vertical**. A horizontal force goes side to side. It also goes forward and backward. When Ben pushed the box across the ground, he pushed it horizontally. A vertical force goes up and down. Together, Ben and his sister pulled the box up off the ground. This was a vertical force. Setting the box down is also vertical.

CHAPTER TWO

Contact Forces

There are many different kinds of forces. Some forces happen when things touch. These forces are called **contact** forces. Most forces are contact forces.

One contact force is called applied force. This force can both push and pull. It happens when a person or object uses force on an object. When Josie moves a chair, she uses applied force. She pulls the chair away from her desk so she can sit down. When she is done, she pushes it back in. Both times she is touching the chair and using force.

Pushing a chair is one example of applied force.

When a person leans against a tree, the tree pushes back.

Another type of force does not cause any movement. This is called normal force. Normal force supports things. It happens when an object is in contact with a **stable** object. For example, Helen sets her lunch tray on the table. The tray pushes down on the table. The table pushes up on the tray. This force can also be horizontal. Drake is tired after running during recess. He leans against a tree. His lean pushes sideways against the tree. The tree pushes back. Neither moves.

Some forces make it harder for things to move. These forces are **friction** forces. Friction happens when one object tries to move across another object. Harper pushes a hockey puck across the ice. The hockey puck slides fast and far. There is little friction between the ice and puck. But if Harper pushes it across grass, the puck does not go as far. There is a lot of friction between the puck and grass.

The weight of an object changes how forces affect it. An object that weighs a lot needs a lot of force to move it. Eva is pulling a wagon. It does not weigh much when it is empty. Eva does not need a lot of force to pull it. When her brother sits in the wagon, it gets heavier. Eva needs more force to pull it.

Weight can also change how fast an object moves when a force is added. Lacey plays soccer with her friends. She kicks the ball as hard as she can. This adds a lot of force. The ball is light. It moves quickly. Clayton helps his mom decorate her garden. He pushes a small statue. It is heavy. He uses a lot of force, but it moves slowly.

A ball will travel a long distance quickly when kicked because it does not weigh much.

CHAPTER THREE

Gravity

Many forces happen when things touch. But some types of forces can happen between things that do not touch. These types of forces happen at a distance. **Gravity** is one type of force that acts at a distance.

Gravity is a force that happens when a **massive** object pulls smaller objects toward itself. Earth is a massive object. Everything on Earth experiences gravity. Earth's gravity pulls things down to its center.

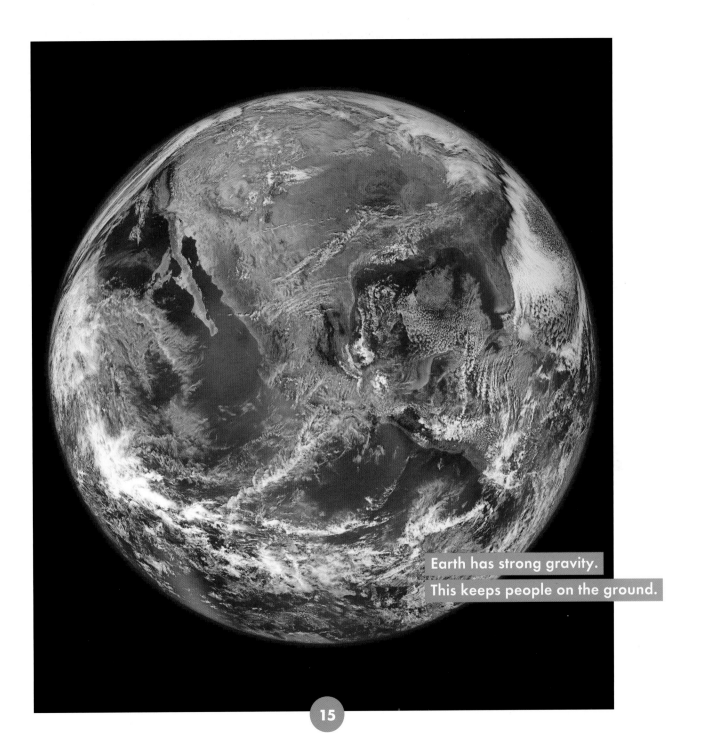

Earth has strong gravity.
This keeps people on the ground.

Without gravity, a basketball would float away.

Gravity happens even when things are not touching. A basketball falls down through a hoop. The basketball is not touching the ground. But gravity still pulls it down.

Gravity affects the entire **solar system**. The sun is even more massive than Earth. The sun's gravity is incredibly strong. It pulls all the planets in the solar system toward it. This keeps them from flying off in space.

CHAPTER FOUR

Many Forces at Once

Often, more than one force acts at a time. Ellen plays softball. She is the pitcher. She pulls the ball back. Then she throws the ball as hard as she can. The ball flies through the air. When Ellen throws the ball, she pushes the ball forward. As the ball flies, the air causes friction. This slows it down. Gravity pulls the ball lower. The batter hits the ball. It flies far out into the field.

Many different forces happen during a softball game.

19

Gravity pulls down on the ball.

The ground pushes up on the ball.

The ball lands. It bounces and then it rolls. As it rolls, the grass pushes against the ball. The friction slows it down. The ball stops. The ball is not moving. But there is still force. Gravity pulls the ball to the ground. And the ground pushes against the ball. The ball stays still because these forces are **balanced**. Both forces have the same strength. They also act in opposite directions. One pulls down and the other pushes up. The forces cancel each other out. The ball stays still. It is stable.

An outfielder picks up the ball. New forces begin to act on the ball. No matter what, some force will always be acting on the ball.

Push vs. Pull

Push	Pull
Happens between two objects	Happens between two objects
Has strength and direction	Has strength and direction
Moves an object away from the force	Moves an object toward the force
Applied force	Applied force
Normal force	Gravity

Glossary

balanced (BAL-uhnssd) Something is balanced when all parts are equal. Balanced forces have equal strength and go in opposite directions.

contact (KON-takt) Objects are in contact when they are touching each other. A tray is in contact with a table.

force (FORSS) A force is a push or pull on something. Pushing a box uses force.

friction (FRIK-shuhn) Friction is a force that slows things down when they rub against each other. There was little friction between the puck and the ice.

gravity (GRAV-uh-tee) Gravity is the force that attracts smaller objects toward a massive object. Earth's gravity pulls objects down.

horizontal (hor-uh-ZON-tuhl) Horizontal means flat or parallel to the ground. Something that moves to the side goes in a horizontal direction.

massive (MASS-iv) Something is massive when it is very, very large and heavy. The sun is massive.

solar system (SO-lar SIS-tim) The solar system is the group of planets that travel around the Sun. Earth is one planet in the solar system.

stable (STAY-buhl) Something that is stable is steady. The table is stable.

vertical (VUR-tuh-kuhl) Vertical means up and down. Something that moves down moves in a vertical direction.

To Learn More

In the Library

Crane, Cody. *Push and Pull*. New York, NY: Children's Press, 2019.

Housel, Debra J. *Forces*. Huntington Beach, CA: Teacher Created Materials, 2015.

Sikkens, Crystal. *What Makes it Move?* New York, NY: Crabtree Publishing, 2020.

On the Web

Visit our website for links about pushing and pulling:

childsworld.com/links

Note to Parents, Teachers, and Librarians: We routinely verify our Web links to make sure they are safe and active sites. So encourage your readers to check them out!

Index